IBTIDA

A THREAD OF FATE

OM PRAKASH BHARADWAJ

Made with ♥ on the Notion Press Platform
www.notionpress.com

To my dear wife.

Contents

Also by Om Prakash Bharadwaj

A Garden Of Verses.

"I was made and meant to look for you, wait for you and become yours forever"

FOREWORD

Ibtida began as more than just words on a page. It started as a feeling, a memory, really, of a quiet moment that, for reasons I could never fully explain, felt monumental. In the middle of an ordinary day, in the busy hallways of life, I saw her. It was the kind of moment that makes time seem to pause, where the world around fades, and you're left wondering if you've just glimpsed something extraordinary. It was in that silence, that single glance, that this story truly began. This book is my attempt to capture what that felt like. It's not simply a collection of poems; it's a journey. A journey through all the little moments and emotions that come with finding someone who feels like home. These pages hold snapshots of the raw, the vulnerable, and the beautiful every heartbeat, every question, and every quiet revelation that love brings. I wanted this book to be real, to feel human and imperfect, because love is exactly that. It isn't always grand gestures or dramatic moments. Often, it's the small things a shared smile, a subtle glance, or the words left unspoken that leave the deepest mark.

As you read Ibtida, I hope you find pieces of yourself in these lines. I hope it reminds you of the beginnings that have touched your heart, the connections that defy explanation, and the beauty in waiting for something real. My wish is that these poems give voice to emotions you've felt but maybe never found the words for, that they offer comfort, warmth, and a reminder that love, in its simplest form, is a story worth telling.

PREFACE

When I set out to write Ibtida, I didn't start with a plan or a structured idea of what this book would look like. It began with memories, emotions, and a desire to trace the steps of a journey that felt both uniquely mine and somehow universal. This isn't just a collection of poems; it's a story told in pieces, with each poem capturing a moment, a feeling, a fragment of something much bigger than words can hold. Writing this book was like walking through each chapter of my own heart, pausing to observe the small details and the subtle shifts that often go unnoticed. Each poem is a reflection of a phase in the journey of love, starting from the very first spark, moving through the quiet understandings, the unspoken hopes, and the depths of connection that words sometimes fail to capture. Unlike many poetry collections that stand as individual pieces, I wanted Ibtida to flow as a continuous story, with each poem feeding into the next, as though you're following a path that unfolds with every page turned. In Ibtida, you'll find that the poems are arranged in phases, each representing a different aspect of love and connection. I wanted readers to feel the progression, to experience the way love grows and deepens, how it matures and sometimes surprises us. The structure of the book is like a journey you can step into a pathway that leads you through those first glances, the shared silences, the waiting, and the realization of a bond that feels almost destined.

This book is different from other poetry collections in that it doesn't just aim to share thoughts on love but to immerse you in a story, a continuous experience that you might relate to in your own way. I wanted Ibtida to be a companion, something you could return to whenever you want to remember the beauty of beginnings, the strength in vulnerability, and the quiet power of connection. My hope is that, as you read, you feel not just the emotions I've poured into these pages but also a resonance with your own experiences a reminder that love, in all its forms, is both simple and profound.

Acknowledgements

This book would not exist without the love and support of those closest to me. To my family, thank you for always believing in me and for your constant encouragement through every step of this journey. To my friends, thank you for being my sounding board, my cheerleaders, and my source of strength. Your patience, insights, and unwavering belief in this book have meant more than I can express. And to her—this story is, in so many ways, a reflection of you. Without you, Ibtida would simply be an idea without heart. Thank you for inspiring these pages and for being the reason this journey even began.

With all my gratitude,

Om

PROLOGUE

It was a strange feeling, stepping into a world so different from the one I knew. I came from a small, familiar place, where everyone knew each other, and life had a rhythm that felt easy to understand. Back in my old school, I was the quiet one, a bit of a nerd, content to keep to myself and get lost in books and studies. I had a solid group of friends guys who felt like brothers, who understood me without words. Talking to girls, on the other hand, was rare, almost unfamiliar territory. Then, I moved to a new school National Center for Excellence, or NCFE. The change was immediate, like stepping into an entirely new world. I was no longer invisible, in fact, it felt like everyone was looking at me. I didn't know what it was. Maybe it was the newness of being a stranger, or perhaps there was something different about me that even I couldn't see. I wasn't used to the attention, the glances, the curious smiles. It was overwhelming, to say the least, to go from the comfort of blending in to suddenly being someone people noticed. Everything felt bigger here the hallways, the faces, even the possibilities. It was like being dropped into a world where the rules I'd known no longer applied, and I was just trying to find my way. This is where Ibtida began, in those first uncertain days at NCFE, where I was just a kid stepping into a story I hadn't yet realized was mine to live.

This book is that journey from that first day, from the glances and the silence, through everything that followed. It's a story of how someone can come into your life and, without even knowing it, change your world.

I

The First Glance

It was my second day at National Center for Excellence, and I was still struggling to find my footing. Everything felt new, too new, maybe. My transfer from the familiar halls of my old school had left me feeling like a stranger in my own skin. This wasn't just about uniforms or new faces; it was about stepping into a world that seemed larger, louder, somehow out of reach. I was a shy kid, reserved to the point of invisibility, and yet, here, I found myself at the center of attention. It wasn't something I had ever asked for. The girls, especially, seemed interested. I noticed their glances, the way they'd whisper to each other, casting curious looks my way. It was strange, unsettling. I wasn't used to it, and part of me wanted to disappear into the background, to slip into the quiet, unnoticed. But the more I tried to withdraw, the more visible I felt. It was like trying to hide in plain sight. On that particular day, the warmth of the afternoon sun filtered through the school's corridors, casting long, lazy shadows. I stood outside the classroom with a friend, half-listening to his words, my mind drifting elsewhere. The usual hum of students surrounded us voices, laughter, footsteps but it was all just noise to me. I was lost in thought, wondering if I'd ever find a place here, if I'd ever belong.

And that's when it happened.

Across the corridor, near the staff room, *I saw her.*

At first, it was just a glance. A girl standing by the balcony, her back partially turned, her hair catching the sunlight in a way that made it seem to shimmer. She was talking to a friend, but her presence pulled at me, like a magnetic force I couldn't resist. I found myself looking at her, drawn in by something I couldn't name. There was a kind of grace in the way she stood, something effortlessly beautiful, like she was in her own world, untouched by the chaos around her.

And then, as if sensing my gaze, *she turned.*

Her eyes met mine, and the world seemed to stop.

It wasn't a casual glance. It was something deeper, something that felt like a spark igniting in the quiet space between us. My heart began to race, each beat loud in my ears, drowning out everything else. *She held my gaze,* just for a moment, but in that moment, everything shifted. It felt like we were the only two people in the corridor, like the universe had orchestrated this single second, this chance meeting. Her friend leaned over, whispered something to her, and *she smiled*—a small, soft smile that seemed to reach right into me. *I felt it*, like a warmth spreading through my chest, a feeling I'd never experienced before. It was like discovering something precious and fragile, something you want to hold onto but fear might break if you even breathe too loudly. I tried to act normal, tried to pull my gaze away, but *I was caught, mesmerized.* There was a softness in her eyes, a depth that seemed to draw me in, making me want to know her, to understand who she was. In that one glance, she had become more than just a girl in the hallway; she was a mystery, a question waiting to be answered. For a second, I wondered if she felt it too—*that strange, electric connection,* the pull that seemed to bind us together, if only for a heartbeat. It was foolish, maybe, to think that a single look could hold so much meaning. But in that moment, *it felt real*. It felt like the beginning of something.

I stood there, rooted to the spot, watching as she turned back to her friend, the moment slipping away as quickly as it had come. She was still smiling, her gaze no longer on me, and I felt a pang of longing, a strange ache I couldn't quite name. I wanted to call out to her, to ask her name, to say something, anything, that would keep her from disappearing. But I stayed silent, caught between the thrill of that brief connection and the fear of breaking the spell. And then, just like that, she was gone. The corridor filled with noise again, the hum of students, the laughter, the footsteps—all of it rushing back in, drowning out the quiet magic of those few seconds. For the rest of the day, her face lingered in my mind.

I replayed the moment over and over, each time feeling that same rush, that same sense of wonder.

It was as if her image had etched itself into my memory, a part of me that I couldn't shake, no matter how hard I tried. Her hair, the way it caught the sunlight, the softness in her gaze, the curve of her smile I remembered it all, each detail vivid, each one a reminder of something I couldn't name. That night, I lay awake, my mind restless, filled with questions.

Who was she?

What was her name?

Would I see her again?

I didn't have answers, but in the quiet of my room, with the world slipping into sleep, I let myself believe, if only for a moment, that maybe.. just maybe.. this was the start of something more. The next day, I searched for her, my heart leaping every time I turned a corner, hoping to catch a glimpse of her. But she wasn't there. The hallway felt empty without her, the day stretching long and silent. I told myself it was just one day, that she'd be back, that this wasn't the end.

But *she didn't come.*Days turned into a week, then two, each one a small ache, a quiet reminder of what I had lost. The memory of her *began to fade,* but only just enough to make it bearable, enough to let me move on, even as her image stayed, a faint imprint in the back of my mind. And then, ten weeks later, I heard her name in passing, a casual mention from someone in class. *She had left,* gone without a word, *transferred to another school.* The news hit me like a punch to the chest, a strange, hollow emptiness settling inside me. *She was gone* just like that, without a chance for me to know her, to even *learn her name.* It felt surreal, like a cruel joke played by fate. I had been given a moment, a single, perfect moment, only to have it taken away before I could understand what it meant. I thought about it often, wondering if it was destiny, if maybe this was the universe's way of making me wait, of teaching me patience. Or maybe it was just a passing moment, a memory meant to stay exactly as it was beautiful, untouched, a glimpse of something I would never have. But deep down, I couldn't shake the feeling that this wasn't the end.

Nazm-e-Dil

-

when our eyes met the world hushed— time slowed, and I, for the first time, felt the earth tilt in the direction of a smile.

Some people are finite,
passing through, fading fast.
But you
you stay, like the sky after rain.

i posted poems
to be seen,
but somehow,
i was always writing for you.

I was the sky, vast and waiting,
and you were a fleeting comet,
gone before I knew to hold you.

some moments
come with no warning,
but leave you
forever changed.

it wasn't just the words
that connected us—
it was the spaces between them.

you liked my words,
but it was your silence
that spoke the loudest.

i was never patient,
but somehow,
waiting for you
felt like the only thing
i knew how to do.

our story started
long before we even knew
we were in it.

the red thread
doesn't ask for permission
it just pulls,
quietly,
until you find your way
to each other.

it wasn’t love at first sight,
but it was love
before i even knew your name.

i didn’t lose you,
i just didn’t know
i was waiting
to find you again.

the best surprises
are the ones
the universe hides
in plain sight.

i wasn’t searching for you,
but somehow,
you were all
i was looking for.

In a single glance,
I saw forever,
But forever passed,
In the time it took to breathe.

the universe has a funny way of making sure
you meet the people you're supposed to.

there's a difference
between being lost
and being found
sometimes,
you have to be both.

The breeze caught your hair,
And with it, my heart,
Tangled in strands of gold,
That the wind could never steal away.

We were just two strangers,
Until the universe decided otherwise,
And suddenly,
You were more than a name I didn't know.

It wasn’t the stars,
Or the sun,
Or the world outside us,
It was just you and I,
In a shared breath.

I watched you smile, and in then the world felt smaller,
Like it belonged only to us.

For a moment,
The ground wasn't real,
My feet touched nothing,
And all that held me was the way you looked back.

You were soft,
But you stirred a storm in me,
One that I never wanted to end.

It was nothing,
And yet,
It was everything,
The start of a story I couldn't wait to tell.

We hadn’t spoken yet, but love doesn’t need words
It just needs a moment and we had ours.

You exist in places you'll never know—in my laughter,
in my silence and in every breath.

One second,
and my life was rewritten
in a glance, in a smile,
in the way you just existed.

I could meet a thousand souls and yet I would only see you,
like a melody thats stuck long after the music stops.

Love has no edges,
no ending, no borders.
You live in me
like water held by the ocean.

I don’t know her name,
yet she lives in every thought.

She glanced my way,
and I forgot the world.

If love is a story,
then this is the prologue
the part where I don't know her name,
where I only know the pull of her presence,
the way she felt like the beginning of something
that has no end.

How can someone be gone
yet feel so close?
How can a memory have weight,
enough to pull me back to that hallway,
to the warmth of her gaze,
to a moment I never wanted to end?

II

The Turning Point

Moving on was easier than I thought. By the time I'd settled into the routines of my new school, the memory of that brief encounter on the balcony had softened, becoming a quiet part of the past. Life around me was lively, vibrant, full of new faces and experiences. The whispers and curious glances from the girls that had once felt overwhelming began to take on a new charm. Slowly, I found myself warming up to the attention, letting it feed a confidence I hadn't known I had. With time, I grew comfortable in my role. I was no longer just the *new guy*—I was someone who stood out. People knew my name, they called out to me in the halls, and I'd catch myself smiling, enjoying the warmth that came with it. I mingled, I laughed, I found myself slipping into conversations with ease, letting the admiration surround me like an invisible cloak. The days moved quickly, one blending into the next, and before I knew it, I was stepping into 12th grade.

Everything about that year felt different. The atmosphere shifted, from lighthearted chatter to the focused buzz of students pouring over textbooks and revision guides. Everyone was talking about the future, about exams and colleges, and I was no exception. The usual laughter in the corridors faded, replaced by the quiet intensity of last-minute study sessions and endless assignments. My days were consumed by my books, and the people around me blurred into the background. I was more focused, more reserved, driven by the pressure of what lay ahead. I still had friends, still exchanged smiles in the hallways, but my mind was elsewhere, tied up in the demands of the year. I didn't realize it then, but life was beginning to shift in ways I couldn't foresee. Then COVID arrived, sweeping through our world like a sudden storm, pulling everyone into an unfamiliar silence. Schools closed, plans halted, and we found ourselves locked within the four walls of our homes, connected only by the glow of our screens. The days became a blur, one indistinguishable from the next, each one marked by a strange stillness. As the lockdown stretched on, I took my next steps from a distance. I applied to colleges, sent off documents, went through the motions of entrance exams, and soon enough, found myself with an offer from MS Ramaiah Institute of Technology. An engineering student that's who I was becoming. But it was a strange start, a disconnected beginning, as my first year of college unfolded online, from my own bedroom.

New faces appeared on the screen, small boxes containing people who, in any other time, would have been classmates, friends. I made a few connections here and there, exchanged a few messages, but it wasn't the same. The friendships felt thin, stretched across the chasm of the internet, barely scratching the surface of what real connection should feel like.

Finally, as the world began to open up again, I set foot on campus in my second year, ready to live out the college life I'd heard so much about. The campus was buzzing with energy, with the thrill of freedom that only comes after being confined for so long. *Parties, late nights,* laughter that spilled into the early hours of the morning-college life was everything I'd imagined and more. I found myself in a new life, surrounded by faces I was learning to recognize, people who seemed genuinely interested in me. I'd never been someone who chased after attention, but here, it came naturally. People gravitated towards me, and I found myself at the center of conversations, the subject of glances and whispered words. I didn't know if it was my looks or something else, but the interest was undeniable. I enjoyed it, basked in it, letting it fuel me in a way that felt almost addictive. Living in a flat near college, away from home, gave me a taste of freedom I hadn't known before. Late-night study sessions turned into *impromptu parties,* conversations flowed as easily as the music, and I was pulled into a world where rules seemed to bend, *where limits felt distant.* I was surrounded by new people, new experiences, and life was moving fast, too fast to stop and think about anything other than the present. I went on trips with friends, road trips to places that felt untouched, where we'd spend hours exploring, laughing, filling the days with stories and moments that felt endless. I'd watch the sunrise from the windows of moving train, feeling the thrill of youth, of being on the edge of something vast and unexplored. Girls came and went, new faces blending into my new life, each one leaving a small, quiet mark before drifting away.

The days felt golden, rich with laughter, each one an adventure I hadn't anticipated. I felt like I was living in a story, one that had no end, no sense of time. The friendships I made were light, easy, and everything about it felt temporary, like pieces of a puzzle that didn't quite fit but made sense in the moment. I was content, caught up in the thrill of it all, letting myself drift along, enjoying each new connection, each fleeting moment. But as third year began, the energy started to shift. The friendships that once felt effortless began to change, and the faces I'd once seen every day started to fade. I started noticing things I hadn't before—the way people talked when they thought I wasn't listening, the double-edged compliments, the glances that seemed less warm, more calculated. There were smiles, but now they felt hollow, and slowly, I began to realize that some of the people around me were wearing masks, their true intentions hidden behind polite words and feigned interest. I could see it in the way conversations would shift, how people seemed interested in being around me only when it suited them. The laughter started to feel forced, and the connections I'd held onto began slipping away. It was unsettling, but also liberating. I found myself surrounded by fewer people, the crowd thinning, leaving only those who genuinely cared. The friendships that remained were real, grounded, built on something more than surface-level admiration. The attention that had once felt so comforting now seemed superficial, shallow, a temporary high that left me feeling emptier than before. I realized that many of the people I had once called friends were more like acquaintances, temporary companions on this journey. And slowly, I became okay with that.

As my third year drew on, the people who had stayed by my side were fewer, but they were true. The conversations I had were deeper, richer, filled with the honesty I'd once thought impossible. I learned to embrace the quiet, the smaller circle, finding comfort in the simplicity of real friendship. The people who mattered were still there, and that was enough. I went through the days with a new understanding of what it meant to have real connections, to be surrounded by people who saw me for who I was, not just what I appeared to be. The emptiness that had once been masked by attention now felt like a space I was learning to fill with something more meaningful. College life had shifted from the rush of popularity to something more grounded, something that felt like truth. And though I still had a wide circle, still enjoyed the laughter and companionship of many, I knew that not everyone was meant to stay. People drift in and out, each one bringing something new, each one leaving a lesson, a quiet mark on the story of my life.

As the third year began to draw to a close, something shifted on campus—a subtle, yet unmistakable sense of urgency settled over everyone. College life, which had once felt carefree and filled with endless possibilities, was beginning to narrow into something more focused, more serious. The laughter and chatter that had once filled the hallways became softer, tinged with the quiet pressure that only grows when the future is on the line. Placement season had arrived, and it brought with it a sense of weight, a reminder that our time here was finite. My friends, the people I had shared countless memories and late-night conversations with, were each on their own path, preparing for a world that seemed vast and unknown. For the first time, I watched as people I'd spent years with began to set their sights on new horizons, getting placed one by one. I could see the relief, the joy, in their eyes as they shared their news, their excitement mingled with a kind of nervous anticipation. But each of their successes was also a reminder of my own uncertainty—a reminder that soon, I would have to make my own leap into whatever lay beyond.

Then, in September, something unexpected happened in the campus—for the first time a Japanese company announced it would be coming to our college for placements. This wasn't just any placement opportunity. It was something entirely new, a chance to step into a world I had always dreamed of, a place I'd held a quiet fascination for. Japan had always intrigued me—the culture, the language, the way it seemed both ancient and modern. The idea of working there, of living there, felt like a door opening to a future I had only dared to imagine. The excitement on campus was palpable; whispers filled the hallways, and everyone seemed to be talking about it, wondering who would get the chance to go, who would be selected. Around 200 to 260 students applied, each one hoping to be among the few chosen to interview with these Japanese companies. But in the end, only 6 people were shortlisted, and somehow, I was one of them. When I saw my name on that list, I felt a mix of disbelief and excitement, a thrill that ran through me, grounding me in a way that I hadn't felt in a long time. Two companies, JMC Japan and Think Laboratory Limited, had chosen me to interview, and the news brought a sense of purpose, a sense of direction that I hadn't fully expected. My interview was scheduled for December 12th, giving me just over a month to prepare, to do everything I could to make this dream a reality. The countdown began, each day bringing me closer, each hour reminding me of what was at stake. For the first time, it felt as though the future was within reach, a tangible thing that I could shape with my own hands. But with that opportunity came a weight, a pressure that was as exhilarating as it was overwhelming. The stakes were high, and I knew this was a once-in-a-lifetime chance, one that could change everything. I stayed up late, poring over notes, reading everything I could about the companies, about Japan, imagining myself there, working, exploring, living the life I had always dreamed of. I wanted this—not just because it was an incredible career move, but because I felt a pull toward Japan, a desire to be part of something bigger, to step into a world that felt both familiar and new.

My friends were supportive, offering encouragement, sharing advice, but there was an unspoken understanding among us that this was different. This wasn't just another placement; this was the beginning of something real, something that carried the weight of responsibility and the promise of a future I had longed for. With each day that passed, the pressure grew, and the anticipation settled deeper into my bones. I could feel it every time I closed my eyes, every time I pictured myself stepping into that interview room, knowing that this was my chance. As the days of passed, I found myself drawn not just to my studies, but to something new, something unexpected—poetry. It had started quietly, almost by accident, a way to put my thoughts into words when the world felt too heavy, too vast. I'd write late into the night, the pages filling with pieces of myself, lines and verses that I'd never imagined putting down. Somehow, the words brought a calm I hadn't known before. With the weight of placements growing, poetry became my way to breathe, to pause, to look inward even as I prepared for the future. The thought of Japan lingered in my mind, filling me with both excitement and nerves, and writing became a way to balance the intensity of it all. As my friends discussed interviews and deadlines, I'd find myself lost in verses, words becoming my quiet escape, a place where I could let go of the expectations and simply be. Between the nights spent preparing and the hours I devoted to writing, a strange peace settled over me—a balance between the dreams I held for the future and the voice I was discovering within myself. The pressure was there, yes, but so was the thrill of creation, the satisfaction of seeing my thoughts take shape on paper.

Ghazal-e-Khayal

I’ve held on to broken things, not because they were mine, but because I feared the empty hands.

We were ships passing in the night,
silent, distant,
leaving ripples that would reach for years.

I thought love would be louder,
a roar, a storm.
instead, it was a whisper, soft and clear.

In a world full of mirrors,
I looked for windows,
a way to see past my own reflection.

My heart is a city of echoes,
empty streets, abandoned voices,
haunted by the ones who never stayed.

I asked the sky for answers,
but it only offered rain,
washing away everything
I thought I knew.

Love arrived like a letter,
signed only with a sigh,
sealed by time,
never opened.

I wore patience like an old sweater,
threadbare, softened by time,
hoping you'd come to find warmth in me.

Life was a painting,
and I, a brushstroke lost in color,
blending into the canvas of days.

Each night was a book,
filled with chapters I'd never read,
yet somehow knew by heart.

The world became a song,
and I, a quiet verse,
learning to hum along.

In quiet hours, I painted my own sky,
each star a dream, each night a page.

With each passing day,
I became a poem, unfinished and raw,
a verse to be read by the wind.

I wore my heart like an old jacket,
tattered yet warm,
learning to feel without fear.

Every new face was a mirror,
showing parts of me
I had yet to meet

Love me gently,
as rain loves the earth
quiet, patient, and persistent
in its devotion.

Love me where I break,
where my edges are jagged and worn,
for there lies the beauty of becoming whole.

I am nothing more than a feather,
drifting, aimless,
until you give me the sky to call home.

With every goodbye,
I lose a little of myself,
leaving fragments in places
you will never return to.

if you listen,
you can hear my heart
in the quiet spaces between waves,
calling out for you.

III

The Cosmic Conspiracy

The third year of college was a blur of deadlines, late-night study sessions, and balancing my new passion for writing. Poetry had become my escape. It felt like the more I wrote, the more I could understand myself, like every word on the page held a part of my heart I hadn't yet discovered. I began posting my poems on Instagram, hoping to share my thoughts with the world, and maybe, just maybe, someone out there would understand the emotions woven into each verse. That was when it happened.

In August, I started to notice something. Every time I posted a poem, there was someone—an account—that liked each one. One by one, she went through every poem, appreciating every word, every thought. And then, after a few days, she sent me a request from her private account. I accepted, curious, but there was nothing to see. No pictures, no posts—nothing to satisfy the curiosity that had suddenly sparked within me. But still, I couldn't stop thinking about her. I didn't know why I wanted her to text me or why I was so eager to see if she liked my poems. Maybe it was the mystery. Maybe it was something deeper. But I found myself waiting. I started posting more often, almost like I was writing for her. With every story, I hoped she'd read it, hoped she'd like it. It became almost obsessive, the way I waited for her interaction, each little "like" feeling like a small moment of connection. And then, on August 31st, my wait was over.

She finally replied to one of my stories. It was a simple picture—me with my nieces. But her response? It was as if she had shattered the quiet space I'd been living in. "*How cute!*" she said. And just like that, everything changed. I was in the metro when I saw her text, and for a moment, the world around me disappeared. My heart was bursting with joy, and I couldn't stop myself from grinning. The metro sped through the city, but inside, I felt like time had slowed, as if the universe was holding its breath, waiting for my reply.

"*Oh thanks, and hey, I'm sorry for replying this late,*" I typed. "*I was too tired and fell asleep.*"

Immediately after hitting send, I cringed. What a stupid response. Overthinking started to take over what if she hated it? What if she didn't reply? But she did reply. We started talking, small conversations at first, and I found myself waiting for her text all day. I had never been one for texting, but with her, it was different. We exchanged stories, shared childhood pictures, and even joked about going to Jaipur together someday. There was something about her that made everything feel so natural, so easy.

And then, one day, I asked, "Where do you live?"

Her reply shocked me: "*I live near your school.*"

My heart stopped for a second. How did she know? I had never mentioned it before. And then, the pieces started falling into place. "Wait," I asked, "how do you know about NCFE?"

"*I went to the same school,*" she said, "but I left in 11th grade."

It was like the world turned upside down. My mind raced, connecting memories and fragments of the past. I asked her again, almost in disbelief, "You left in 11th? When?"

And that's when she said it. "*I left two days after joining.*"

I froze. She was *the girl*—the same girl from six years ago. The one whose eyes had met mine just long enough to leave a mark, a mark that had never really faded. I couldn't believe it. After all these years, after everything, she had come back into my life quietly, unexpectedly, like some cosmic twist of fate. The realisation hit me like a wave. *It was her*. The same girl I had watched walk away all those years ago was now here, talking to me, liking my poems, and unknowingly tying herself back into my life. It felt like the universe had been conspiring all this time, waiting for the perfect moment to bring us back together.

In that moment, I couldn't help but think of the ancient Japanese legend of the red thread of fate—the invisible string that connects two souls destined to meet, no matter the time, place, or circumstance. It felt like this was it. That red thread, which had been tugging gently at our hearts all along, had finally brought us together again. It was more than just coincidence. It was cosmic, like the universe had woven our lives together in ways I couldn't begin to understand. I was overwhelmed with emotion—shock, joy, disbelief. Everything felt surreal. "*You're the same girl*," I finally managed to type, my fingers shaking as I hit send. And in that moment, I realized that we were always meant to find each other again. The red thread had never broken, just stretched, patiently waiting for us to cross paths once more.

Shariq-e-Hayat

-

Our lives were chapters in separate books,
until fate folded the pages,
binding them together.

There you were
a stranger I somehow knew,
a memory waiting to surface.

We were tied by something
neither of us could see,
yet felt with every step closer.

Years fell away,
and suddenly, we were back,
as if time had merely paused,
waiting for us to catch up.

I had tucked you away, like a letter I couldn't throw out,
afraid I'd lose a piece of myself.

You reappeared quietly,
slipping back into my life
like a song I hadn't heard in years.

We were lines in a poem,
separated but unfinished,
waiting to rhyme again.

I didn't need to look for you,
fate had its way of bringing you back,
one small moment at a time.

There was a thread between us,
so fine we didn't notice,
yet strong enough to pull us together.

What we had,
it lived outside of time,
a love that waited patiently to be found.

I felt the weight of stars align,
as if the universe had stitched us
into its fabric,
just for this moment.

I had carried you all this time,
a quiet presence in the corners of my heart.

I thought you were gone,
but my heart had been waiting
without knowing why.

In every line I wrote,
a piece of you hid,
waiting for you to find it.

What we have doesn't need words;
it's written in looks,
in the spaces between sentences.

We're bound by threads of memory, woven by time,
and knotted by chance.

In my quietest moments,
I had wished for you,
not knowing you'd heard me.

We came back to where we started,
the thread unbroken,
the story unfinished,
waiting for us to begin again.

I looked at you and felt it all the days, the years,
the way you were always there.

Our hearts sat patiently,
in a waiting room built by time,
until fate called our names.

You came back to me like a whisper,
soft, familiar,
carrying the hope of years.

We may have walked away,
but that thin thread held on,
knowing we'd find our way back.

You were the ghost in every room,
the shadow in every verse,
haunting me without knowing.

Meeting you again felt like coming home,
to a place I hadn't known I'd left.

You were the sentence I left incomplete,
the thought unfinished,
waiting for the words to return.

I looked at you,
and for the first time,
the world made sense.

You were hidden in every poem,
waiting to be seen,
woven into my every word.

Our story didn't end,
it simply waited
outlasting years and silence.

Perhaps we were held
in the gentle palms of fate,
safe until the right time.

Somehow, in my heart,
I had always known
you'd find me again.

Across miles, across time,
you were always there,
waiting in the spaces I couldn't fill.

They say stars tell stories,
and I think ours
was written in their quiet light.

You were a stranger,
and yet, everything about you felt
like something I'd never lost.

Seeing you again felt like a promise kept,
a long-awaited homecoming
wrapped in silence.

Every poem I wrote was a bridge,
leading me back to you,
one verse at a time.

You hid in the corners of my memory,
in verses I didn't understand
until you returned.

In the end,
you were the one who stayed,
even when you weren't there.

IV

Ibtida

I didn't know what it was at first the feeling that started like a whisper but grew louder each day, turning into an urge, a silent wish, something I couldn't name, but I felt it deep inside. Every time we talked, I could feel myself slipping, wanting something more. It wasn't just curiosity anymore, not just about knowing her favourite books or the places she wanted to travel. No, this was something else. I wanted to be part of those plans. I wanted to meet her. I knew she loved Van Gogh. The way her eyes would light up when she mentioned his name, as if she were talking about an old friend. The artist who painted flowers with such vivid colours, capturing their life even as they withered. And so, like anyone struck by a feeling they didn't understand, I found myself learning everything I could about Van Gogh, his life, his work, the tragic beauty in his strokes. I remember laughing at myself because I wasn't an art lover, never had been. But with her, I wanted to be anything, everything she admired. There was going to be an exhibition of his work in Bangalore, and I told myself this was my chance. I made up my mind. I'd take her there, and in the dim light of those paintings, I'd get to know her better. It was silly, none of it made sense to me, but I'd convinced myself this was it. This was the moment, the perfect excuse to be close to her. I asked her, a little too eagerly perhaps, if she'd like to go with me. She agreed. The way her excitement mirrored mine, even if just a little, was enough to keep me awake that night, replaying our conversation over and over in my mind. We set a tentative date for September 7th, and I started counting the days. I hadn't felt this alive in a long time. But just as things seemed to align, life did what it always does—it threw a twist my way. She told me, one evening, almost in passing, that she was planning to go to Amsterdam. She was leaving on September 9th, just two days after we were supposed to meet. She said it casually, not realising what it did to me. The words settled like a weight on my chest, heavy and immovable. Amsterdam, of all places—the city of Van Gogh, the city that called to her in ways I couldn't compete with. She was going to visit her sister, just for a few months, she said. She'd be back by December 9th. December felt like a lifetime away. I knew I should have been happy for her; she was excited, after all. But in my heart, all I could feel was an ache, a hollow sadness that gnawed at me. I had only just found her. We hadn't even had the chance to meet, and already she was slipping away. That night, I lay in bed, staring at the ceiling, thinking about her in a way that went beyond words. I wanted so badly to see her before she left. To have something, some memory, to hold onto while she was away. But as the days passed, our plans kept falling through. Life got in the way. She got busy with last-minute preparations, college placements kept me tied up, and before I knew it, the 7th had come and gone. We never made it to the exhibition.

And that's when something inside me shifted. I had never been one to believe in miracles, in fate, or in praying for something. But for her, I started to do all of it. Quietly, privately, I began to pray—not for Japan, not for my future. No, I prayed for her. I prayed that she'd come back. I prayed that fate, the universe, whatever power held the threads of our lives, would bring her back to me. Japan was secondary, a mere backdrop to the life I imagined with her in it. I wanted stability, yes, but only because it meant that I could have a future where she was a part of it. I didn't tell anyone about it, didn't say it out loud. It was *my secret*, my silent wish. Every day, I found myself thinking of her, imagining what it would be like when she returned. I started to dream about a life where she was always there, a part of every small and big moment. I even thought about marriage, though it seemed absurd, thinking so far ahead. But I couldn't help it. She was in my every thought, my every hope. In September, during Durga Puja, I began to pray in earnest. I kept Navratri for the first time, fasting and offering my hopes up to something bigger than myself. Me, the atheist who had never believed in God, was suddenly reaching out to a force I couldn't see, asking for something that I couldn't put into words. I prayed every day, lit candles, offered flowers, whispered my wishes into the quiet. I didn't know if it would work, but I did it anyway, hoping that somehow, the universe would listen. I even fasted on Diwali, feeling foolish but desperate, clinging to the idea that maybe, just maybe, this would make a difference. As the days turned into weeks, I found myself adapting to this strange new routine waiting for her messages, talking late into the night, learning new things about her with each conversation. She told me about her love for art, about her dreams of studying for her master's in Amsterdam, her fascination with the canals, the tulip fields, the endless museums she wanted to visit. Each day, it felt like she was painting a new part of herself, revealing different versions I hadn't seen before. And every time she shared something, I found myself falling a little deeper, caught in this silent pull, this quiet thread that bound us together. The ache of knowing she was miles away only grew stronger. But in some strange way, the waiting brought us closer. She'd call unexpectedly, her voice a soft song in the stillness of my room. Sometimes, she'd ask, "*Did I disturb you?*" and I'd laugh, shake my head, trying to keep the excitement out of my voice. "*No, not at all,*" I'd say, though I knew I'd drop anything, anyone, just to hear her speak. We talked about her days in Amsterdam, about the places she visited, the things she saw, and each word became a new thread weaving us closer.

October rolled in, and though the wait felt endless, it was filled with moments I cherished. She'd call sometimes just to say hello, sometimes with stories about the cafes she visited, the art she had seen. Her voice was a lifeline, a reminder of the connection we were building even from so far away. And slowly, I realised that I was falling. Not just in the way people say, in passing, but truly, deeply. I knew it in the way I counted down the days to her return, in the way her voice lingered in my thoughts long after we'd said goodbye. I knew it in the way I could imagine nothing but her, as if the rest of the world had faded into the background, leaving only us. And still, every night, I prayed. It had become second nature to me by then, this silent ritual. Before sleeping, I'd close my eyes and picture her, wherever she was, hoping she felt the same pull, the same longing. I asked for one thing only, that when she returned, we'd find our way to each other, that fate wouldn't keep us apart this time. Japan had become secondary; it was a future I dreamed of, but only because it meant I'd be able to build something steady, something I could share with her. November arrived, and with it, a growing anticipation that felt almost unbearable. The days felt slower, each one stretching into eternity as I waited, hoping for news, for a sign. Then, one evening, as I sat alone, she messaged me with news that made my heart race. *"I'll be back on December 9th,"* she said. I read those words over and over, letting them sink in. December felt close and far all at once, a promise on the horizon. I remember that night vividly, lying awake, my thoughts running wild. I couldn't help but imagine what it would be like to finally see her, to meet her face-to-face. My mind played out endless scenarios, each one more vivid than the last. I pictured her smile, the way her eyes would light up when she saw me. I imagined us sitting together, talking about all the things we hadn't been able to say over the phone, the things that had been waiting in the spaces between our words. As the days drew closer, I started preparing in small, quiet ways. I bought a new shirt, practiced things I might say, though I knew I'd forget them the moment I saw her. I even kept a list of small reminders for her simple things like drinking water, not trusting strangers, taking care of herself. It was silly, maybe, but I couldn't help it. I wanted to be there for her, even if just in small ways. And then, finally, November 30th arrived, and with it, the news I had been waiting for. She messaged me, telling me she'd returned the night before, a surprise she hadn't revealed. I could hardly believe it, I must have read her message ten times, each word filling me with a joy I hadn't felt in years. She was here. She was back. The waiting was over, and we were finally going to meet. That day felt surreal, a dream I was living in real-time. I got ready with a nervous excitement that made my hands tremble. I wanted everything to be perfect. I remember standing in front of the mirror, applying a bit of shimmer to my face, a foolish attempt to look my best, though I knew it didn't matter. But still, I wanted her to see me at my best, wanted to make an impression, even if I felt like a nervous wreck inside. I left for the café in Indiranagar, hoping to find a flower shop on the way, but time was against me. There were no flowers, nothing to add to the moment, but I told myself it didn't matter. She was the only thing I needed. As I reached the café, my heart was pounding, each beat louder than the last. I stood outside, hands clenched, thoughts racing. *What would I say? Would she feel the same way? What if she didn't?* The doubts crept in, but before I could dwell on them, my phone buzzed.

"*Where are you?*" she asked, her voice light but carrying a warmth I could feel even over the phone.

"I'm... outside," I said, trying to keep my voice steady.

"*Outside... where?,*" she replied.

I looked up, and there she was, standing just inside the café, waiting for me, her gaze searching. She noticed me and stepped outside, and for a moment, I just stood there, taking her in, feeling the world slow around us. She was right there, close enough to touch, close enough that I could see the softness in her eyes, the slight curve of her smile. Without thinking, I walked towards her, closing the space between us, and as we met, I wrapped her in a hug. It was instinctive, a moment I hadn't planned but felt right, like every step we'd taken had led us to this embrace. As she leaned into me, I caught her scent—soft, floral, and warm, something comforting yet completely captivating. Her fragrance wrapped around me, familiar and new all at once, as if I had known it all my life. I wanted to hold onto that moment forever, the feeling of her close, the quiet rush of knowing she was finally here. I held her a moment longer, savouring everything about it, the softness of her hair, the warmth of her presence, the scent that seemed to hold memories I hadn't made yet. Finally, reluctantly, we pulled apart, and I looked at her, a smile breaking out despite the thousand words I couldn't say. We walked inside, and everything felt surreal, like a dream I'd stepped into. The café was a quiet space, the sounds of clinking cups and low conversations fading into the background as we found a corner by the window. She glanced around, her gaze curious, but when she looked back at me, her smile held a shyness that made my heart skip. We sat down, and for a moment, there was a gentle silence between us, filled with unspoken things. I wanted to tell her everything—how much I'd thought about this moment, how she had become the centre of every wish and prayer. But instead, we began to talk about simpler things, about her trip, her stories from Amsterdam, the places she had seen. She spoke about her sister, the laughter in her voice a song I could listen to forever. As she talked, I couldn't help but watch her, the way she moved, her beautiful eyes, the way her hands gestured as she described the canals, the museums, the paintings that had caught her eye. She was like a painting herself—every detail vivid, every small detail a new colour I hadn't seen before. And then, as if sensing the quiet intensity in my gaze, she looked at me and smiled, her cheeks tinged with the softest blush.

"*I got you something,*" she said, her voice soft, almost shy.

From her bag, she pulled out a notebook, its cover adorned with the delicate, intricate blossoms of Van Gogh's Almond Blossom. She held it out to me, and for a moment, I just stared, taken aback by the thoughtfulness, the way she had brought a piece of her world to share with me.

you didn't just bring me a gift
you brought me pieces of your heart,
stitched together in art,
in petals, in a painter's quiet dreams.

I took the notebook from her, carefully, like it was something precious, something I wanted to keep safe. "Thank you," I said, my voice barely more than a whisper, the weight of the moment settling over me.

"*It's my favourite,*" she said, glancing at the cover.

"*I thought... you might like it, too.*"

Her words were tentative, hopeful, and I nodded, words failing me. She had brought me a piece of herself, something meaningful, and in that moment, I realised just how deeply I felt for her. The hours passed like minutes, and we were lost in conversation, sharing stories, laughing, exchanging memories as if trying to make up for the months we had been apart. She told me about her life, the things that made her laugh, the dreams she held close. And I told her about my dreams too, the things I had never shared with anyone. It felt natural, easy, like we had known each other for a lifetime. As the evening wore on, the light outside began to fade, casting a soft glow over us, and I felt the weight of the moment, the way everything seemed to fit together, like pieces of a puzzle finally falling into place. I wanted this memory to last forever, the warmth between us, the laughter, the quiet understanding. When it was time to leave, I found myself hesitating, reluctant to let go of the moment, the new feeling, her presence. We walked around the street near the cafe clicked photos and then we took an auto to her place, the evening breeze cool around us, but inside, I felt a warmth I hadn't known before. We talked about small things, making plans we hadn't yet committed to, as if we were testing the idea of a future together.

Finally, we stood outside her apartment, a gentle silence settling over us. I wanted to say something, to tell her what this evening had meant, but the words felt too heavy, too clumsy to capture the feeling. So instead, I smiled, and she smiled back, and for a moment, we simply stood there, caught in the quiet magic of this beautiful evening.

sometimes,
the loudest things we feel
are the ones we never say
held in the stillness
of shared glances.

As I walked away that evening, my heart was full, overflowing with an emotion I couldn't name, but felt deeply. She was more than just someone I liked; she was someone I could see a future with, someone who made me believe in things I had never considered before. *She was magic*, the kind of magic that doesn't announce itself but lingers quietly, waiting to be discovered. In the days that followed, I replayed that evening over and over in my mind, each detail as vivid as the moment it happened. The way she had looked at me, the warmth of her hug, the sound of her laughter. It became my most cherished memory, a moment I held close, something that I knew would stay with me forever. And as the days turned into weeks, I found myself longing for more, for the simple comfort of her presence, for the quiet conversations and the laughter we shared. She had become the centre of my world, the one thing that made everything else seem insignificant. I knew, in the quiet of my heart, that I had fallen for her, and there was no going back.

Ibtida-e-Ishq

I learned the art of waiting,
one prayer at a time,
and found a new kind of faith
in the quiet ache of loving you.

I can feel you,
like a heartbeat I never knew I had.

I imagine us in small moments
morning light through an open window,
the warmth of your hand in mine,
a future that feels like home.

I've woven you into silence,
the words I dare not say
held between breaths,
between heartbeats.

For you, I believe in miracles, in a universe that bends just so we might find each other.

You're the light I carry through the dark, a glow that doesn't fade
no matter how long I walk alone.

Every prayer, every whispered hope
I offer them all, wrapped in the softest corners of my heart.

We stood there, on the edge of something unnamed, a threshold. I hoped you'd step over with me.

I keep you here
pressed against the pages of my heart,
like a flower I can't bear to let go.

You're in every thought, a thread I keep pulling until there's nothing left of me that isn't tied to you.

I count the days,
not in time, but in heartbeats,
in all the ways I know
I'd wait forever.

You are here,
even in your absence,
a presence that fills the spaces
no one else could reach.

Loving you isn't loud,
it's the gentlest of things,
a quiet devotion
that feels like coming home.

Even miles away,
you pull me,
an invisible thread
I don't want to break.

In the quiet, I find you,
a calm beneath the longing,
a stillness that feels
like grace.

I didn't know I was missing anything
until you filled all the empty spaces
I'd been keeping safe.

You're a sky full of stars,
a map I trace in silence,
each light a promise
that leads me back to you.

I wait, not with impatience,
but with a heart full of knowing
that love like this
is worth every second.

You carry a light that makes everything softer, like dusk settling over a quiet lake.

Your memory wraps around me,
like a familiar coat,
warm and worn,
perfectly fitting.

I reach for you
in the quiet hours,
where longing grows soft
and hope takes its place.

You left something with me
not a word, not a touch,
but a presence that lingers,
like the last note of a song.

For you, I've become someone new,
like petals unfolding in the sun,
unaware of their own beauty
until someone sees them.

I hold you close,
a silent prayer,
a devotion whispered
only to the night.

I've travelled a thousand thoughts
just to find you,
lost and found
in the same heartbeat.

In every story you told,
I saw a piece of myself
uncovered, like a secret
we both somehow knew.

I stay grounded,
even when you're far,
because I know my heart
has already found its home.

Every time you spoke,
I felt a ripple
through the quiet of my life,
a soft echo that never faded.

No matter where you go,
some part of you stays,
a whisper in the air
I can't ever leave behind.

If fate had hands,
it would be yours
gently resting in mine,
like we were meant to arrive here.

You were the song
I knew before I heard it,
the line of poetry
I'd been waiting to write.

I love you in a way that has no beginning, as if you've always been here, as natural as breathing.

I find pieces of you in all the small things the light at dawn,
the quiet at night.

In this world, I found you,
a soul that feels like mine,
and I will hold this knowing
for all the lifetimes to come.

I believe in us,
like the sun believes in dawn,
knowing that even the darkest night
will bring you back to me.

V

The Propasal

Since we first met on November 30th, I'd felt like I was caught in a dream, each moment with her blurring the line between reality and something more. Every time we saw each other, every laugh, every glance, only drew me deeper, until I could no longer deny it because she was *the one.* It wasn't just her smile, or her laugh, or the way she'd listen to my stories as if they mattered. It was her presence, the way she made everything feel... *right.* By the time December 20th arrived, I knew it was time. I was ready to ask her to be mine, to take that leap, no longer content with silence or subtlety. I planned it carefully, imagining each detail. A bouquet of roses, 25 to be exact. Real, vibrant red roses, each chosen with a thought of her. But nestled right in the middle, I placed a single artificial rose, one that carried a hidden meaning. Inside this rose was a ring, small and glistening, a pink emerald that held a quiet, hopeful promise. I thought of it as our own little secret, something that would tell her just how much she meant to me, how deeply I had fallen.

With my heart pounding, I took the bouquet in hand, rehearsing everything I wanted to say. The words felt fragile, teetering on the edge of my lips as I made my way to her. She sat there, waiting, her face lighting up as I approached. I could see the curiosity in her eyes as I held the bouquet out to her. She took it gently, her gaze soft, and I watched as she held it, wondering if she'd notice the single rose that wasn't like the others. I thought she'd see it right away, that she'd laugh and point it out. But she didn't. She simply held the bouquet, her fingers brushing over the petals, completely unaware of the little secret hidden within.

I couldn't help but smile, caught up in how effortlessly she could be both perceptive and unaware, somehow capturing the charm and innocence that made her... *her.* And so, as she held the roses, lost in their scent, I took a breath, the world narrowing down to just the two of us. Slowly, I knelt down on one knee, my gaze never leaving hers, my heart bare, vulnerable, each beat a reminder of everything I wanted to tell her.

"*I love you,*" I said.

The words coming out softer than I had rehearsed, but honest, grounded, carrying every feeling that had been building inside me. She looked down at me, her eyes widening just a bit, a look of surprise mingling with something I couldn't quite place. She opened her mouth, then closed it, her gaze shifting between me and the bouquet, almost as if she were searching for an answer somewhere in the petals. I waited, feeling the world slow, the air around us thick with anticipation.

"*Om...*" she whispered.

Her voice trailing off, leaving her thoughts unreadable, a mystery hanging between us. Her gaze softened, holding mine, and in that silence, a thousand words seemed to pass between us, words that neither of us spoke. And there we stayed, suspended in that quiet moment. She stood there, bouquet in hand, and I knelt before her, waiting, caught between hope and uncertainty, wondering what her answer would be, what the next moment might hold.

To Be Continued...

This story doesn't end here. I've left it at a moment, where her answer remains untold. The next part of this journey will come in the fall of 2026, when I'll return to finish the story as it was meant to be told. Until then, thank you for being a part of this beginning.

The Parijat.

Take my hand
Take my whole life, too
For I can't help falling in love with you
-Elvis Presley

www.ingramcontent.com/pod-product-compliance
Lightning Source LLC
LaVergne TN
LVHW091254150826
845673LV00006B/1413

* 9 7 9 8 8 9 6 1 0 1 5 9 8 *